CRETE
ON OLD
MYSTERIES

CRETE

Victor J. Kean

NEW LIGHT ON OLD MYSTERIES

EFSTATHIADIS
GROUP

EFSTATHIADIS GROUP S.A.
14, Valtetsiou Str.
106 80 Athens
Tel: (01) 5154650, 6450113
Fax: (01) 5154657
GREECE

ISBN 960 226 224 9

© **Efstathiadis Group S.A. 2001**

All rights reserved; no part of this
publication may be reproduced, stored in a
retrieval system or transmitted, in any form
or by any means, electronic, mechanical,
photocopying, recording, or otherwise, without the
prior permission of Efstathiadis Group S.A.

Printed and bound in Greece

To Lela and Andreas

Contents

List of Illustrations

Foreword

1	Heraklion	15
2	Knossos	19
3	The Snake Goddesses	25
4	Lustral Areas	31
5	Double-Axe of the Minoans	35
6	Leaping of the Bull	39
7	Art of Fresco Restorer	45
8	Giant Pithoi - The Potter's Art	49
9	Marks of the Minoan Masons	53
10	Ancient Writings	57
11	Lassithi and the Cave of Zeus	61
12	Palace of Malia	65
13	Gournia - Minoan Town of Artisans	69
14	Vasiliki, Pre-Minoan Settlement	73
15	Minoan House of Chamaizi	77
16	Palace of Zakros	81
17	Myrtos - Early Minoan Town	85
18	Gortyn - Roman Capital of Crete	89
19	Palace of Phaistos	93
20	Summer Palace at Triadha	97
21	Frangokastello	101
22	The Samaria Gorge	105
23	Palaechora	109

List of Illustrations

Figure A	Map of Crete	10
Plate 1	Heraklion Harbour	14
Plate 2	Knossos - Past and Present	18
Figure B	Plan of Knossos	20
Plate 3	Attendant	24
Plate 4	Snake Goddess	24
Plate 5	Snake Goddess	24
Plate 6	Dancing Women	26
Plate 7	Women at Worship	26
Plate 8	Ornate Double-Axes	34
Plate 9	Miniature Double-Axes	34
Plate 10	The Bull Rhyton	38
Plate 11	Two Bull-leapers	38
Plate 12	Bull-leaper (Ivory)	40
Plate 13	Bull-leaping fresco	42
Figure C	The Kneeling Bull	40
Figure D	Prince of the Lilies	44
Figure E	Giant Pithoi	48
Plate 14	Human figure Mark	52
Plate 15	Trident Mark	52
Plate 16	Double-Axe Mark	54
Figure F	Twin-arrows and D-Axe Marks	54

Figure G	Ancient Writings	56
Plate 17	Windmill (Lassithi Plain)	60
Plate 18	The Fertile Lassithi	60
Plate 19	Bee Pendant	64
Plate 20	Leopard Pommel	64
Plate 21	Minoan Houses	68
Plate 22	Octopus Vase	68
Figure H	House on the Hill	72
Plate 23	Vasiliki Ware	72
Plate 24	Chamaizi Hilltop	76
Plate 25	Minoan House (Chamaizi)	76
Figure I	Plan of Zakros	80
Plate 26	Ceremonial Vase (Zakros)	80
Figure J	Plan of Gortyn	88
Plate 27	Laws of Gortyn	88
Figure K	Plan of Phaistos	92
Plate 28	Bowl (Phaistos)	94
Plate 29	View of Triadha	96
Plate 30	Pithoi Magazine (Triadha)	96
Plate 31	Castle of Frangokastello	100
Plate 32	Lion of St. Marks	100
Plate 33	The Samaria Gorge	104

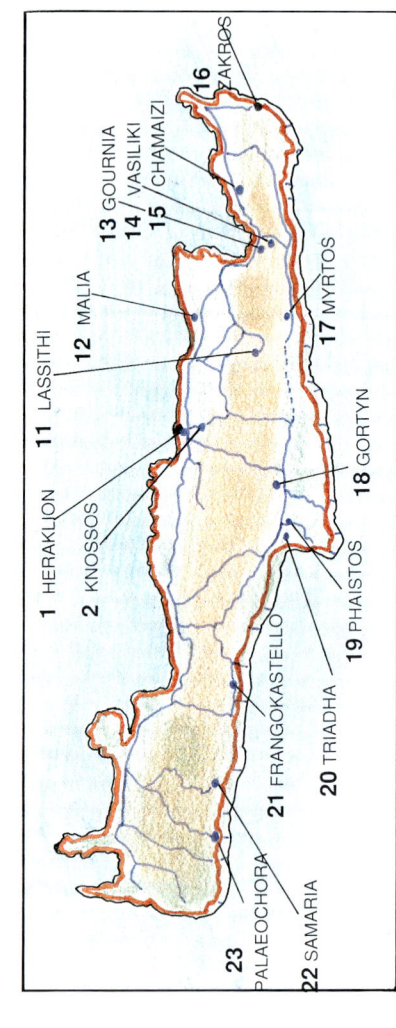

Fig. A. Map of Crete.

Foreword

Visitors to the island of Crete are soon captivated by the mixture of past and present that waits around every corner. Traces of past glories can be found at some of the most beautiful places on the island, for the ancient Minoans also appreciated pleasant locations in fine landscapes.

At first glance many of the more well-known sites appear to be nothing more than a collection of stone walls;yet once - long ago these thronged with people. The walls echoed to the sounds of the mason's hammer as he chipped out the sign of the double - axe. The grunts and groans of men lifting massive blocks of dressed stone into position, mingled with the laughter of countless generations who once lived in these now silent places. In the cool rooms of the palaces children played, whilst out in the surrounding fields the workers struggled to tease the fruit of grape, olive and corn from the fertile soil.

Rich memories of this unique past have been unearthed by the archaeologists and are now on public display in the Heraklion Museum. Yet many of these finds still retain an air of mystery. Exquisite figurines of half - clad females entwined with live snakes. Bronze double-axes too thin to have been used in anger. Athletes vaulting over fearsome bulls, watched by crowds of rouged and red-lipped females. Strange sights to our modern eyes.

In the pages that follow many of these age-old mysteries are considered afresh, whilst some of the lesser known sites of Crete, many of them off the normal tourist route, are to be found. All will provide the reader with unforgettable memories of this lovely island.

Plate 1. Heraklion Harbour.

1 Heraklion

Almost exactly mid-way along the northern coast of the island stands its largest city, Heraklion. The modern town with broad promenades and narrow streets is surrounded by some 5 km of thick, defensive wall built by the Venetians. Four gates built at intervals around this outer wall allows access to the countryside.

Besides the ancient harbour, adjacent to the modern port, stands the Venetian castle overlooking the many fishing boats which shelter within the shadow of its walls. Bathed in clear sunlight, this area is a delight for all photographers (Plate 1).

The main street which climbs up from the harbour into the town is 25th August Street, so named to commemorate the Holy Day of St. Titus. The ancient church of St. Titus with its reconstructed loggia, stands on the left hand side of the road as we climb the hill. Here we can also see the Venetian church of St. Mark built in 1239 A.D. On the right hand side will be found El Greco Park and the square of Platon Kalegron.

A delightful and popular focal point for the many visitors to the town is found at the Morisini fountain. Grand Master Morisini led the defence of the city against the Turks in 1645; a heroic stand which lasted some 22 years. Today the heraldic lions guard the spring waters which gush from the fountain. The 'Mayndani', as the city centre is known, is a natural meeting place. Book shops, jewellers, souvenir shops and many tavernas cluster around. A number of narrow streets fan out in every direction. From the central traffic lights, the well-known market street (1866 Street) will delight most visitors.

Fresh meats, fruits, vegetables and wines are readily available. Roasted coffee adds its delightful aroma to those of the many souvlaki and fish dishes which are prepared to order. Heavy aromatic spices, almonds and lemonade and an abundance of sweet delights are displayed for the would-be purchaser.

A must for all visitors to the island is the world renowned Archaeological Museum in Xanthoudidou, just off Platia Eleftherias. It is near the outer wall on the eastern side of the city. This museum contains almost all the movable finds from the various Palaces and lesser sites with which the island abounds. A visit to the Museum will whet one's appetite to venture through the island and find the places from where these treasures originated.

Plate 2. Central Courtyard - Knossos Past and Present.

2 Knossos

"One of the ninety towns is a great city called Knossos"
Homer c. 700 B.C.

For many years as the workers in the fields around the hill of Kephala, some 5 km south of Heraklion, struggled to till the soil, they uncovered objects of great age. Many of these were small sealstones with curious designs, which the local people made into necklaces. Larger pieces of broken pottery were thrown to one side to make way for the planting of crops.

Not until 1878 when a local merchant, Minos Kalokairinos began to excavate the area, did the first traces of the ancient city of Knossos come to light. Kalokairinos uncovered two of the storerooms of the Palace full of giant storage jars (pithoi), which he found were surrounded by massive stone walls.

The site was eventually acquired by Sir Arthur Evans in 1900. When the first serious excavation began, Knossos was buried under 10 metres of soil. The buildings which were uncovered had suffered the effects of countless earthquakes over the centuries, and were a mass of collapsed stonework. Once uncovered, the soft

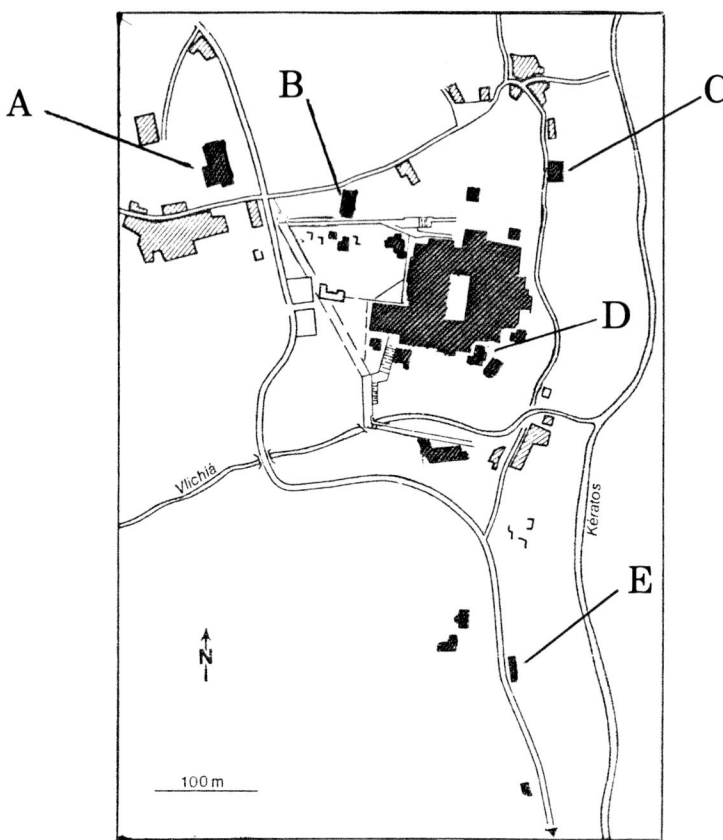

Fig. B. Site plan of Knossos.

gypsum stone which had been used in many parts of the Palace needed protection against the elements, otherwise it would have quickly deteriorated.

It is to the eternal credit of Sir Arthur Evans and his chief assistant D. Mackenzie, that the restoration of the Palace was undertaken with such urgency. The original columns had been fashioned from the wood of the Cypress tree. These once grew in profusion throughout the island. Evans, restored the columns using concrete shaped in faithful copy of the originals.

In the first three years, Sir Arthur uncovered all the main buildings of the Palace. He continued his work for the next 40 years, bringing to the attention of the world the full wonder of the Minoan culture.

Estimates of the number of people who lived in Knossos at the peak of its history vary from between 30,000 to 82,000. The fact that Knossos was not a fortified city exemplifies the general air of peace and tranquillity which pervades through the Minoan Culture. This peaceful aspect if reflected throughout Minoan art. The Minoans had no need for weapons of war, nor did they glorify heroic deeds on distant battlefields.

These and many other aspects of Minoan life were so divorced from the European cultures, that scholars still struggle to find acceptable explanations for some of the objects which have been found. Bronze double-axes of many different sizes with thin fragile blades. Large areas for ceremonial washing with no supply of water or drainage facilities. Small statuettes depicting half-clothed females, their arms entwined with snakes. Scenes of dangerous rituals combing athletic prowess in the company of fearsome looking bulls. These mysterious aspects of Minoan life can be seen by the visitor to Knossos and the Heraklion Museum. (See Chapter 1)

Here at Knossos, we can walk through the Palace corridors and delight at the restored grandeur of the buildings. Thanks to the tremendous work by the British School of Archaeology, we can now walk down the oldest road in Europe marvelling at its condition. We can walk across the Central Courtyard (Plate 2) and stand before the oldest throne (Mycenaean) still in its original position. We can see for ourselves the open stone drains and connecting pipes with their parabolic curves at the corners designed to minimize overflow, which provided some basic hygienic conditions for the inhabitants. Climbing the stairways, we can stand before the coloured wall paintings (frescoes) and visit the Queen's Megaron with its vivid blue dolphins sporting on the walls, and wonder at the sheer magnificence of the whole Palace complex.

Aside from the main Palace building, other smaller excavated buildings are well worth a visit (Fig. B).

These include: -

A) The Little Palace - At the end of the oldest road or 'Royal Way', either side of which are the remains of the foundations of Minoan houses. Columns with evidence of convex fluting were found here.

B) The House of Frescoes - so named from the stack of frescoes which were found neatly piled one atop the other. These fragile pieces of painted plaster seemingly carefully placed as if waiting to be found (See Section 7).

C) The Royal Villa - From this building the King, seated on the small throne set in an alcove in the west wall, could communicate with his advisers whilst remaining unseen. From the balcony, the religious sports could be watched.

D) The House of the High Priest - which lies to the south of the main buildings, was a holy sanctuary. Between two pillars stood a stone altar in front of which were two stands for double - axes.

E) The House of the Chancel Screen - Here in the Megaron stands a raised dias on which was originally a minor throne. A Pillar crypt can be seen on the western side of the house, whilst an example of a 'lustral area' can be found close to the entrance (See Section 4).

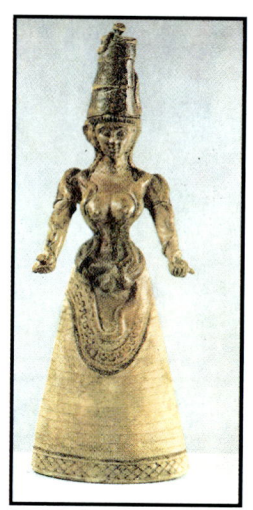

Plate 3. Attendant (Faience).

Plate 4. Snake Goddess (Faience).

Plate 5. Snake Goddess (Ivory).

3 Snake Goddesses

The Temple Repositories (Storerooms) of the Main Palace of Knossos were discovered in its West wing. In this area were found two large cists built below the level of the floor, in which were unearthed three shattered figurines. With painstaking care these tiny statuettes were pieced together and repaired. The results can be seen in Case 50 - Room IV in the Heraklion Museum. These are the famous Snake Goddess and her two attendants.

The restoration of these exquisite works of art was aided by the knowledge gained from many other finds. Similarly dressed females can be seen on various rings and sealstones found on the island. Study of these revealed that these statuettes were of a female diety (Goddess) and her two attendants. If one studies the dress of the three figures, it can be seen that those worn by the attendants are slightly less ornate than the dress of the Goddess herself. All have the same open-fronted bodice which leaves the breasts exposed. A distinctive feature of Minoan court fashion. Around each arm can be seen the entwined body of a snake. The head of the snake has curled under the arm and back over the shoulder. Its head lies menacingly close to the naked breast (Plate 3). The

Plate 6. Dancing Women from Isopata.

Plate 7. Worshipping Women from Mycenae.

most famous of the Snake Goddesses (Plate 4) stands in a commanding pose with arms outstretched, thus emphasising the naked bosom. In each hand a writhing snake is held high. The tight waist band with the flounced skirt and small apron beneath, is highlighted by the close-fitting bodice with its half sleeves.

A further example of the Snake Goddess made in ivory and gold is now in the Boston Museum of Fine Arts (Plate 5). Gold bands decorate the flounced skirt which has a gold belt around the waist. Gold armlets contrast with the uncovered arms of the figure. The ultra narrow waist, which was artificially constricted, helps to accentuate the fullness of the breasts. Two snakes with body and tails curling around the lower arms of the Goddess, rear upwards.

Two gold signet rings on which are shown other females dressed in similar fashion, deserve our attention. The first of these shows four bare-breasted females (Plate 6). A tiny figure, considered to be a deity, appears to be flying towards the other females who are performing a ritual dance in a floral landscape. The two females on the left raise their arms in a gesture of welcome. Wrist bracelets and armlets with hanging beads can be seen. One of the females has a string of beads entwined in her hair and cascading down her back. Found at Isopata, this ring can also be seen in the Heraklion Museum.

The second gold signet ring was discovered at Mycenae on the Peloponnese, and is now on display in the National Archaeological Museum in Athens (Plate 7). This shows six Goddesses in an act of religious worship all displaying their breasts. In the centre of the scene a double-axe of religious significance can be seen (See Section 8).

Other examples of the same bare-breast fashion include a terracotta figurine from the island of Keos, wearing a plain long skirt down to her ankles with two flounces around the slim waist.

On the famous Phaistos Disk (Case 41. Room III) in the Heraklion Museum, the symbol of the Woman is also shown in this typical Minoan female dress.

Much comment has been engendered by these displays of semi-nudity, which have been interpreted as either signs of female emancipation or subtle refinements of eroticism. Others have suggested that this was the normal dress of Minoan females, though it was almost certainly limited to the confines of the Palaces.

Let us consider the mental attitude required to handle and control live snakes, albeit non-poisonous ones. This would require many hours of training in order to overcome what would be for many, a natural loathing of these reptiles. This inherent loathing is locked in our genetic memory and recalls days long past when the fear of snakes was a safety precaution. How then would the spectators or worshippers view such a spectacle.

Deep within the darker reaches of a Minoan temple where the cold air from the earth chills the breath, and the light of the sun is rarely seen, all sounds of the world outside are silenced by the sheer thickness of the stone walls. The Snake Goddess gliding forward out of the shadows into the faint light, the snakes curling and gliding over her bare skin. Forked tongues darting and searching as those fearsome shiny bodies writhe in her hands. After such a display, should we be surprised if many of the worshippers were convinced that the Snake Goddess possessed supernatural powers?

Evidence to support the theory that the complete uncovering of the breasts was not common to all females even within the Palace, can be seen in 'La petite Parisienne' fresco. Here the fashion is to thinly cover the bosom with diaphanous material. This style of dress though less emphatic than before, nevertheless still echoes the same aura of feminism.

4 Lustral Areas

The act of lustration or ceremonial washing, is a ritual performed before or during religious rites. It has been practised by many cultures both ancient and modern.

Visitors to the Palaces of Knossos will discover a number of rooms designated as 'Lustral areas' or chambers. They will also note that other areas called Bathrooms, appear to be very similar to the 'Lustral areas'.

It was Sir Arthur Evans who originally specified which rooms within the Palace were considered by him to be bathrooms, and which areas were used for ritual lustration. He was quite clear in naming as bathrooms those with a purely domestic function, whilst those areas associated with ritual became lustral areas. Later archaeologists called these simple differentiations into question.

R.W. Hutchinson (1950) "They cannot be bathrooms because they have no drains and piping, and because they are lined with gypsum which dissolves in running water'.

J.W. Graham (1968) after an in-depth and detailed consideration of the controversy declared, "The question should not have been whether these rooms were bathrooms or lustral chambers for they were both at once."

Curiously, these and many other scholars who have considered this matter seem to have overlooked certain basic facts. It is not necessary to have *piped* water or in-built drains in order to wash in a bathroom.

"Next came another maid with water in a splendid golden ewer. She poured it out over a silver basin so that I could rinse my hands."   "The Odyssey" Homer 700 B.C.

Nor if one exercises a certain degree of care, is it necessary to concern oneself about the material used in the walls and floors. The use of gypsum throughout the Palace of Knossos has been queried by many due to its poor wearing qualities. However, a nearby quarry made its provision easy to obtain for the original builders, and it also had the advantage of being more easily worked than limestone or marble.

A feature of the lustral areas are the steps which lead down into bottom of the chamber where the ceremonial washing took place. This descent took the adherent closer to the Earth Mother, thus adding to the feeling of reverence in that particular place.

Plate 8. Ornate Double - Axes.

Plate 9. Miniature Double - Axes.

5 Double-Axe of the Minoans

From the large, thin bronze double-axes which now stand in Room VII of the Heraklion Museum to the tiny incised double-axes which adorn the blocks of dressed stone at many of the Palaces, the sign is both a symbolic guardian of the sanctity of the areas where it is found and a symbol of religious significance.

Living on an island which had enjoyed many centuries of peace and with their shores protected by the Minoan fleet, the people had no need for weapons of war. Even the few swords which have been found are richly decorated and were obviously only for ceremonial use.

In many caves on the island and particularly at the caves at Psychro (See Section 11) and Alkahori in Central Crete, numerous bronze double-axes of various sizes were found hidden in the crevices of the cave roof (Plate 8).

Many of the double-axes are covered with decorative filigree designs. One particular axe having tiny symbols thought by some to be similar to those found on the Phaistos Disk.

The decorative panels of the sarcophagus found at Triadha which tells much about the burial customs of the

Minoans during the time of Mycenaean control, shows double-axes on long poles standing besides the altars.

The fashioning of these symbolic double-axes in bronze, a semi-precious metal, suggests that the Minoans were willing to put a high value upon their devotions. For bronze, a mixture of copper and tin which had to be obtained from Cyprus or even further afield, would have had to be exchanged for quantities of wool or olive oil.

Plate 10. Bulls Head Rhyton.

Plate 11. Two Bull-leapers.

6   Leaping of the Bull

From the grey mists of legend which tell of Europa, mother of King Agenor being carried on the back of a bull to the awesome stories of the Minatour, half man and half bull; the bull was considered throughout Minoan Crete to represent strength and power.

Withing the enclaves of the Minoan Palaces, there were brave young men and women who were willing to risk their lives in order to display their dominance over this animal. These athletic feats were performed in the belief that such dominance would endow the bull's human tormentor with some of its attributes.

The inner dignity of this noble beast is captured in a masterpiece of artistic talent, seen in the form of the fine serpentine rhyton found at Knossos (Plate 10).

The impression of an agate seal showing two bull-leaping athletes in a combined performance (Plate 11) is just one of the many examples found on Crete in which this daring sport is depicted.

Fashioned in ivory, the slim-bodied athlete has been captured in mid-flight (Plate 12) this artifact can also be seen at the Heraklion Museum.

From the 'Bull Leaping" fresco from Knossos (Plate

Plate 12. Bull leaper (Ivory).

Fig. C. The "Kneeling Bull".

13) we can see just how the act of leaping the bull was performed. The slim female standing in front of the bull is shown grasping its horns, and is being lifted up from the ground by the sheer strength of the bull's neck muscles. A second female stands behind the bull to assist in controlling her companion's landing. The male athlete has somersaulted through the air and landed on the bull's back.

There is no doubt that the event of bull leaping was performed at all the major Minoan palaces. The Central Courtyards at Knossos, Phaistos and Malia were all used for these events. Some structural evidence exists which show how the bull was confined to the Courtyard, and was prevented from escaping into the surrounding palace apartments.

J.W. Graham identified a blind step in the north west corner of the Courtyard at Phaistos as the stone platform from which the athletes leapt over the bull, as shown in the 'Kneeling Bull' gem (Fig. C). Graham proposed the idea that the athlete would wait for the bull's approach whilst standing on the step. When the bull knelt in submission, or tried to climb onto the stone step, the athlete would leap over its back. Since there is no evidence that the bull was killed after these events, constant repetition would ensure that the bull would perform this manoeuvre on cue.

When considering the athletic feats of the young persons, both male and female who performed the dangerous activity of leaping the bull, two salient facts should be appreciated.

Firstly, the stature of both Minoan males and females was smaller than today's modern sizes. The average

Plate 13. Bull-leaping fresco from Knossos.

height of a Minoan male has been quoted as about 1.6 m. (5ft. 3ins). Their straight shoulders and thin waists are a feature of most human representations. Indeed, the 'Priest-King' (Fig. D) appears to have a 30 cm. (13 in.) waist! One can accept therefore that these trained Minoans were extremely nimble and agile.

The second important fact is that the bull was not trained in the same way as a Spanish fighting bull. It would not therefore charge on sight at the slightest movement. Nevertheless, the sport of bull-leaping was still extremely dangerous. The sharp horns could cause severe injury which would sometimes have proved fatal.

Fig. D. "Prince of the Lilies".

7 Art of the Fresco Restorer

Whilst the difficulties encountered by the excavators of the buildings of the Palace of Knossos were of great magnitude, the finer art of the fresco restorer was not without its problems.

For these were really wall paintings rather than frescoes. They had been applied to the plaster of the wall after it had dried and not whilst still wet. The colours were mixed with a binding agent of plaster and applied quite thickly.

In Room XIV at the Archaeological Museum at Heraklion, the recovered fragments of the "Prince of the Lilies" from the corridor of Procession, can be seen against the artistic conception by Edouard Gillerion of the whole of the original figure (Fig. D).

At Knossos, a full-size replica adorns the walls above the actual place where the fragments were found, thus allowing visitors to appreciate how the fresco looked in Minoan times. Sometimes called the "Priest-King', the fresco undoubtedly shows a royal personage; hence the crown of peacock feathers.

Whilst the profile of the face is the work of the restorer it is not, as some have suggested purely a figment of the artist's imagination. The very first fresco to be recovered from the site, known as the 'Cup-bearer', was the original Minoan profile from which Gillerion took his model.

In addition to the feathered crown, the chest and well-muscled arm, left thigh and calf were recovered from the original fresco. The ultra-thin waist could be deduced from the taper of the chest and from the many other portrayals of Minoan youth which have been found.

Fig. E. Giant Pithoi.

8 Giant Pithoi - The Potter's Art

Visitors to the Minoan palaces at Knossos, Malia and Phaistos will not fail to notice the giant pithoi (storage containers). They were produced in red, brown, green and black and used by the Minoans for the storage of olive oil, wheat and lentils. They are often found in 'magazines', the name given to the area containing rows of pithoi.

It was the use of these giant pithoi for the bulk storage of large quantities of olive-oil, that contributed to the eventual destruction of many of the palaces.

Olive-oil was used by the Minoans as a soap substituted, a skin conditioner and as a fuel for their stoves and oil lamps. Yet the hazard of storing inflammable liquid in such quantity and in close proximity to their living quarters was not appreciated. At Malia, the magazine could hold some 23,000 litres of liquid, whilst at Knossos it has been calcuated that some 246,000 litres could be stored. Yet once these containers had been smashed either by earthquake or human intervention, the olive oil flooding from these large magazines, once ignited caused a terrible conflagration.

Various examples of the decorative art of the potter

can be seen. The Minoan love of the free-running spiral design which emulates the waves breaking upon the shore, can be found in profusion. Many petalled rosettes, a design often associated with Royalty encircle some of the pithoi. A decorative lily plant decorates the giant pithoi from Malia (Fig. E).

Common to most of these storage containers, some of which stand over 2 m. in height, is the potter's clever attempts to create the illusion that these giant pithoi were transportable. Small mock handles have been moulded onto the outer faces, though who could ever use them?

Decorative imitation ropework sometime with finer interlacing strands completes the illusion. Though the truth was that many of these giant pithoi were made by the potter in the position that they are now found.

With the use of a small footstool, an example of which was found at Phaistos and long handled ladles, the contents of the pithoi could be recovered.

Plate 14. Representation of Human Figure. (Phaistos).

Plate 15. 'Trident' Mark (Phaistos).

9 Marks of the Minoan Masons

Numerous examples of these marks inscribed on blocks of dressed stone by the Minoan masons can be found at the Minoan palaces and houses throughout the island.

The interpretation of these designs and of their significance has provoked much debate amongst scholars of archaeology.

The fact that some of these signs have been found on blocks still waiting to be moved from the quarry site, have lead to the conclusion that they were a form of building aid. These would have enabled certain blocks to be located in selected positions in the finished buildings.

At the Palace of Phaistos, the 'Human figure Mark' (Plate 14) is an example of a rare mason's mark. It is believed to represent a human being. The example of the 'Trident', also found at Phaistos is a long way from the sea (Plate 15). Whilst one of the largest of the mason's marks is the 'Thunderbolt' (72 cms) also found here.

Of all the various signs to be found, the sign of the double-axe is the most numerous. On the two pillars of the Pillar Crypt to the west of the Central Courtyard at Knossos, some twenty-nine of these particular signs can

Plate 16. Double-Axe Mark (Knossos).

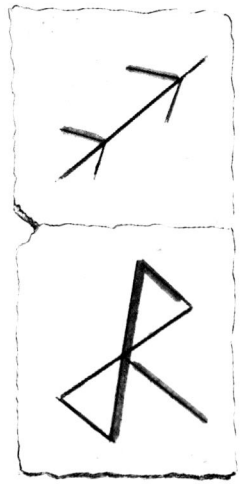

Fig. F. 'Twin-Arrows' and Double-Axe Marks (Peristeria).

be seen. Both at Malia and Zakros, these signs are also in the vicinity of religious shrines. Whilst on the north wall of the Palace of Knossos can be found another clearly incised example (Plate 16).

The mark of the 'Trident' on the blocks of the Sea Gate at Knossos suggests a strong nautical connection, though this sign can also be seen on either side of the gateway leading to the Royal Temple Tomb. The Palace of Malia also displays the 'Trident' along with 'Stars' and other designs.

Evidence of the migration of artisans and masons after the destruction of Minoan Crete around 1450 B.C. can be seen at Peristeria on the Peloponnese. At the entrance to the Royal Tholos Tombs can be seen the rare 'Twin-Arrow' mark with the 'Double-Axe' mark (Fig. E).

With the exception of the 'Double-Axe', many of these signs are the signatory mark of individual masons or teams of masons.

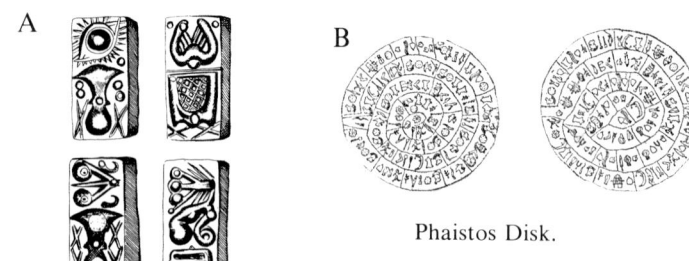

Phaistos Disk.

Inscribed sealstones.

Linear A tablet from Triadha.

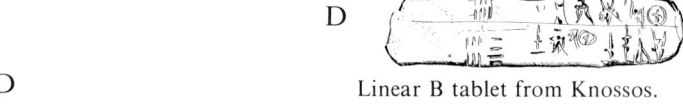

Linear B tablet from Knossos.

Linear B tablet from Knossos.

Fig. G. Ancient writings.

10 Ancient Writings

Much fascination and controversy has been caused throughout the academic world by the attempts to interpret the various symbols found on sealstones, tablets and disks throughout Crete.

Recognized as the early attempts at written communication, these various writings presented an intriguing puzzle to the philologists.

The earliest group of symbols, and those which first caught the interest of the young Arthur Evans, he called 'hieroglyphic' on the assumption that they based upon a similar concept to the script from Ancient Egypt.

Evans published a Table of these Cretan hieroglyphs or conventionalized pictographs as he called them, having collected some 135 different examples (A).

The symbols found on the Disk from Phaistos (2000-1740 B.C.) and which it is now accepted are a mixture of ideograms and pictograms, were possibly derived from the earlier symbols (B). Two stumbling blocks have frustrated many of those who have tried to decipher the Disk.

Firstly, there was always argument as to which way the symbols were to be read until H.D. Ephron (1962) on purely mechanical grounds, established that it was 'printed' from the centre outwards to the rim.

Secondly, many of those scholars who tried to decipher the Disk, did so using the 'Table of Symbols' published in the "Palace of Minos" by Sir Arthur Evans, unaware of the pictorial errors it contained.

The third group of symbols are now known as Linear A. Most of the clay tablets bearing these symbols were found at the Palace of Zakros and at the Summer Palace at Triadha (C). Though certain pieces of pottery from Thera, Kos and Melos also have a few of these signs (2000-1400 B.C.).

Lastly, the script known as Linear B (1450-1200 B.C.) which was eventually deciphered by the late Michael Ventris in conjuction with Chadwick. He proved them to be an archaic form of the Greek language (D). On the island of Crete this script was only found at Knossos. On the Greek mainland examples have been found at Thebes, and on the Peloponnese at Pylos and Mycenae.

Though it was hoped that the decipherment of Linear B would throw light on the life of the inhabitants of Minoan Crete, it was not to be. Most of the surviving tablets are lists of goods, animals or quantities of seed.

However, the names of certain Greek Gods, Zeus, Athene and Poseidon and place names such as Pa-i-to for Phaistos, Ko-no-so for Knossos and A-mi-ni-so for Amnissos could be read using the phonetic values assigned by Ventris.

As was to be expected, many other philologists and archaeologists disagree with the Ventris/Chadwick decipherment though they offer no acceptable alternatives.

Plate 17. Windmill on the Lassithi Plain.

Plate 18. The fertile plain of Lassithi.

11 Lassithi and the Cave of Zeus

The road which turns to the south from Hersonissos winds its smooth way up towards the Lassithi mountains. Gentle bends ease the gradual climb from the coast towards Seli just beyond the village of Krassi. Here one can obtain refreshing lemonade as the road reaches its highest point some 1100 m. above sea level.

Stretching out like a natural carpet, the plain of Lassithi: an almost flat intensively farmed area lies below. Yellow triangles of ripening corn are interposed with dark green olive trees. White goats and black donkeys crop the sweet grasses (Plate 18).

In every direction, the famous white-sailed Lassithi windmills can be seen stirring lazily in the soft breezes. Fewer now than in days gone by, these ancient sails turn in the air drawing crystal clear water from beneath the surface of the plateau to be stored in concrete water containers. (Plate 17)

The water table is constantly fed by the underground rivers from the Dikte mountains. From the earliest times this life-giving water has nourished the soil.

The one road which encircles the Lassithi plain, eventually leads in either direction to one of the most revered shrines on the island. The Diktian Cave at Psychro.

Ancient legend tells how Rhea, heavy with child came to this place and climbed the steep side of the mountain, before descending into the deep cave which lies hidden within its bulk. Here she gave birth to Zeus, God of all Nature.

Today one can still descend into the 100 m. deep cave following the footsteps of the early Minoans who worshipped here for centuries past.

In almost complete darkness, save for the guttering flames of thin yellow candles which shimmer on the surface of the clear water pool at the bottom of the cave, images of the past cast their spell across the reflecting surface of the water. This natural mirror has reflected the faces of thousands of reverent worshippers over the years.

The deep womb-like cave filled with cold, clear air chilled by the mountain, captures the primitive atmosphere. In this timeless place, the world outside is completely forgotten.

Hundreds of votive offerings were discovered amongst the crevices. Knives, double-axes, statuettes and rings were found high in the cave roof.

Today, patient sure-footed donkeys can be hired to carry one up the well-trodden path to the cave entrance. Here candles can be purchased and local guides hired for the descent into the depths.

Plate 19. Bee pendant from Malia.

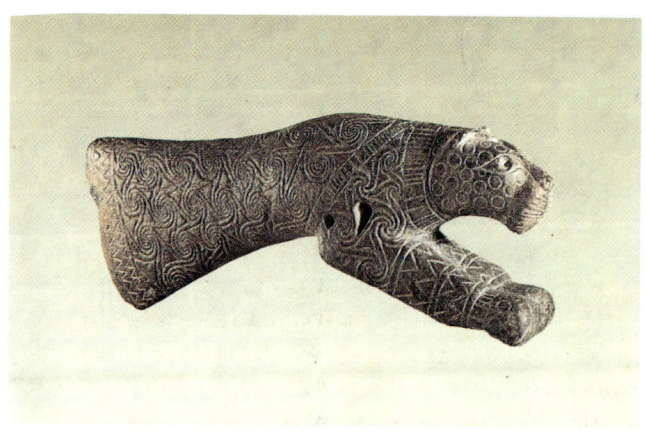

Plate 20. Leopard sword pommel.

12 Palace of Malia

Secure in the knowledge that her shores were well guarded by the Minoan fleet, the Palace of Malia was unfortified. The site of the palace is clearly sign-posted on the northern coastal road.

Constructed from locally found sandstone and ironstone, the Palace of Malia, though lacking in the grandeur of Knossos or Phaistos, still retains its own particular charm.

Arriving at Malia, one can walk along the stone paved path known as the Processional way which crosses the Western Court towards the North Entrance. A giant pithoi stands like a silent sentinel besides the path. Directly ahead is the north-east magazine block.

Turning right through the North entrance, one walks across the North Court to the Court of the Tower. The leopard pommel (Plate 20) and two other ceremonial swords were found in this area. The Pillared Hall and the Ante-room lie to our left . The Central Courtyard is but a few steps away. It was here that the Bull leaping events took place.

In the centre of the courtyard can be found the remains of a sacrificial altar upon which animals were sacrificied to the Gods. Beyond the flights of poorly sighted theatre seats, and further across the courtyard towards the south-west corner, the intriguing 'kernos' can be seen. This stone display dish with its 34 shallow hollows, was filled with various seeds, fruits and plants in a Minoan harvest festival.

To the south of the Palace can be found eight large storage containers; the granary where the produce of the fields were kept for the winter months.

Returning north, we can walk through the Corridor of the Pithoi magazines (See Section 8), at the end of which is the Archive Room of the Palace. Slightly to the north-west will be found a 'Lustral Area' (See Section 4).

East of the courtyard was a two-storeyed building with balconies and columns and further storage magazines.

The beautiful example of gold granulated work known as the 'Bee pendant' was found in one of the tombs between the palace and the sea. Showing two bees either side of a honeycomb, its design is similar to certain Egyptian jewellery (Plate 19).

The history of the Palace of Malia follows that of both Knossos and Phaistos. All were severely damaged around 1730 B.C. and rebuilt. Malia did not survive the effects of the destruction of Thera which followed the volcanic eruption of that island around 1450 B.C.

Plate 21. Minoan Houses in miniature. (Knossos)

Plate 22. Octupus Vase from Gournia.

13 Gournia - Minoan Town of Artisans

Situated within easy reach of the sea some 19 km. beyond Agios Nikolaos, the settlement of Gournia blends in with the slopes of the hill upon which it is built.

Overlooking the Bay of Mirabello, the town was built some 4000 years ago and lies at the narrowest part of the island. Here it served as a trading town between the ancient ports on the south coast and the northern towns.

The houses which are known to have been two storeyed, were probably similar in appearance to those shown in the miniature models found in Knossos (Plate 21). The houses were built close together with outside stairways to the upper floors.

Gournia is composed of a myriad of cobbled streets linking the various houses. Many of these were used by artisans, craftsmen, carpenters and potters who supplied the inhabitants of the island's palaces with the results of their labours.

The workshop of the carpenter was identified by the sets of bronze saws which were unearthed, whilst opposite was found the potter's workshop. An exquisite example of the potter's skill is the 'Octopus Vase' found in Gournia (Plate 22).

On the summit of the town is a Minoan mansion, close by the agora - public meeting place. In this area were found the storage magazines. Limestone drainage channels can be seen throughout the town. In what appeared to be a public religious shrine, a small figurine of a Snake Goddess and a Minoan double-axe were found.

Gournia is considered to be the earliest example of an European town. Its narrow streets and dense living areas were engulfed around 1450 B.C. probably as a result of the volcanic destruction of Thera (Santorini).

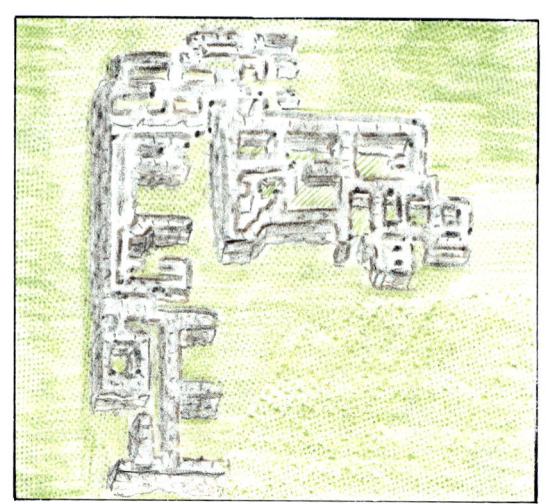

Fig. H. House on the Hill.

Plate 23. Sample of Vasiliki Ware.

14 Vasiliki - Pre-Minoan Settlement

Turn south at the junction towards Hierapetra and travel 3 km. to the minor junction signposted to Vasiliki. The ancient site lies above the road some 300 m. on the left when approaching the modern village.

Known as the "House of the Hill", this once red-stuccoed residence was surrounded by other dwellings separated by paved streets, now lost beneath ploughed fields and olive trees.

Excavated in 1904, this house of many rooms (Fig. H) was made of straw-filled bricks with beam strengthened walls. At least one upper floor was used as living quarters. The ceilings were made of plaster of clay set in reeds.

The potential dangers of storing large quantities of olive oil in buildings made of materials so easily ignited, were not appreciated by the inhabitants of Vasiliki. The conflagration which swept through this pre-Minoan house, was of such intensity that it reached temperatures which almost petrified the stone columns supporting the upper floors. The wooden beams disappeared in the flames leaving traces of ash deposit in the wall sockets.

Much distinctive pottery was found during the excavations, which is now known as 'Vasiliki Ware'

(Plate 23). Blades made of the volcanic glass known as obsidian, and imported from the island of Melos were also found.

The house was destroyed around 2200 B.C. and left abandoned.

Plate 24. Chamaizi hilltop.

Plate 25. Minoan House at Chamaizi.

15 Minoan House of Chamaizi

Heading eastwards along the north coastal road towards Sitia, and having passed through the village of Exo Mouliana, look out for the blue and white sign on the right-hand side of the road reading, ΜΙΝΩΙΚΗ ΟΙΚΙΑ ΧΑΜΑΙΖΙΟΥ.

Situated on top of a steep hill, the Minoan House of Chamaizi commands the surrounding countryside in all directions (Plate 24). Such an advantageous setting ensuring that the inhabitants could not be approached without forewarning.

The Minoan house which has been dated to the Middle Minoan period follows an oval plan which is unique on the island. It follows the natural shape of the hilltop.

The walls of the house are some one metre thick and still stand one and a half metres high. A tribute to the original builders. Slightly less thick are the room dividers at right-angles to the outer perimeter wall. The main entrance to the house is in the south east corner (Plate 25), and leads to the central courtyard which was unroofed and thus provided light to the various rooms which adjoined it.

In the very centre of the house, a deep walled pit some three metres in depth and some two metres in diameter can be found. In the opinion of Xanthoudidis, the Greek archaeologist who originally excavated the site, this pit was a cistern in which many broken pieces of votive statues were found.

Xanthoudidis also discovered various bronze double-axes and saws. Room 4 of the Museum at Agios Nikolaos contains the movable finds from Chamaizi.

The base of an outside stairway which led to the upper floor of the house can be found. A fire and sacrificial altar were also unearthed.

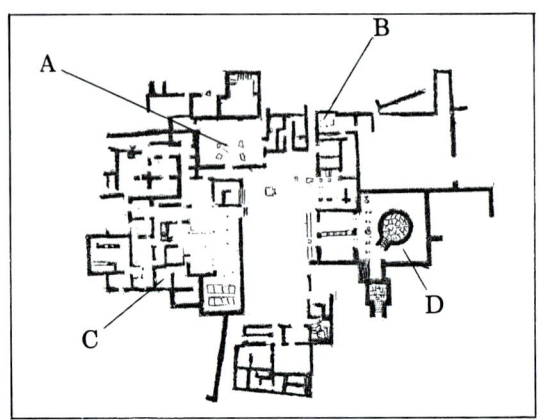

Site plan of Zakros (after N. Platon).

Plate 26. Ceremonial vase from Zakros.

16 Palace of Zakros

Dr. N. Platon, one-time Director of Heraklion Museum, discovered the Palace of Zakros in 1961, by searching at favourable places throughout the island. Such is the visual splendour and beauty of the site at Zakros, that one can understand the Minoan's choice.

Built around the Central Courtyard, the palace complex consists of the King's apartments to the east (B), close to a circular pool. This was fed by a fresh water spring within a collonaded courtyard (D). A kitchen (A) with cooking implements, lay to the north of the dining room. To the west are cult rooms, archives and a treasury. Here were found ingots of bronze from Cyprus, and elephant tusks from Syria. In the archives were discovered tablets inscribed with Linear A script (See Section 10). The recovered treasures from the palace included many ceremonial vases (Plate 23), rock-crystal rhytons, gold pendants and jars and chalices made of both obsidian and marble.

As the first light of the rising sun heralds the dawn of a new day, it rises between the headlands of the bay of Zakros. The prevailing north-west wind wafts over the hills that surround the palace and the town, to flatten the waves in the bay. Lying in the protective shelter of the mountains, the Minoan inhabitants enjoyed an ideal climate. The town's people lived in houses to the north of the palace.

That fateful day in 1450 B.C. when the skies over the bay of Zakros darkened and the air filled with a thick blanket of choking ash, was to be the last time that anyone would live within the palace. Attempts would have been made to flee up into the hills and take refuge in the caves high in the valley. The people never returned. Such was the thickness of the ash-fall that no one ever came to search out the treasures of the palace.

Apart from the archaeological interest, the bay of Zakros is an ideal bathing beach and is well worth a visit. A limited number of rooms are available for overnight accomodation. Local tavernas cater for visitors to Zakros.

17   Myrtos - Early Minoan Town

A small road sign with faded white lettering on a blue background, directs one's attention to the archaeological site at Ancient Myrtos. Though from the position of the sign nothing can be seen of this unique Early Minoan village, known since classical times as Phournou Koryphe. The Hill of Kilns.

It lies some 70m. above the level of the road on a cliff escarpment close to the sea, and some 2 km. east of modern Myrtos.

Spread over an area of some 1800 sq. m. this early settlement is a mass of small rooms (3m × 3m) which were well-built, roofed with plaster and fitted with numerous storage cupboards.

Large pithoi produced by the local potter within his workshop which is thought to be the earliest in the Aegean, and much Vasiliki Ware was found. Wine making was proved by the discovery of pressed pips and grape skins.

According to Prof. Peter Warren who played a leading role in the discovery and excavation of the site, this tightly integrated society was foremost in the weaving and dyeing of cloth.

In the potter's workshop eight clay disks, flat on one face and convex on the other proved to be the rudimentary models of the potter's wheel.

A remarkable find in this Early Bronze Age site was a squat vase shaped in human form. A cult figure with red painted eyes and two long thin arms clutching a miniature jug. The spirit of weaving and water.

Like the House on the Hill at Vasiliki the people of Ancient Myrtos fled their village and the site was destroyed by fire. Never re-occupied, the site remains an Early Minoan time-capsule.

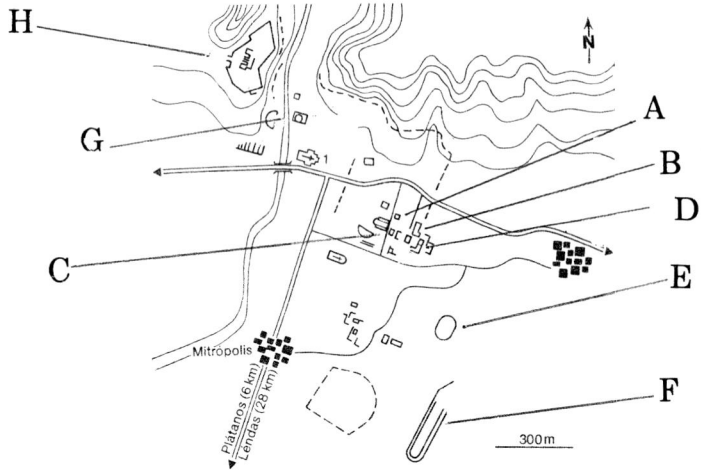

Figure J. Plan of Gortyn.

Plate 27. The Laws of Gortyn.

18   Gortyn - Roman Capital of Crete

With apparent disregard for the intrinsic value of the site of the Roman headquarters at Gortyn, the modern asphalt road from Heraklion cuts a broad swath through its heart. On either side of the road lies the remains of this once important town.

Large sections of wall stand amongst the olive trees. Plain and fluted columns which once supported the elegant roofs of the Temples of Isis and Seraphis stand in ploughed earth. (A) Everywhere shards of Roman pottery give proof to the activity of the now forgotten populace. The Praetorium (B) and the Temple of the Apollo Pithios (C) now serve as a makeshift enclosure for the solitary donkey. The Nymphaeon (D) lay close by.

The complex of Roman buildings which also included an amphitheater (E) and a stadium (F) were the headquarters of the Roman occupying forces dating from the time of Emperor Trajan (A.D. 98-117). From this administrative centre, the Roman High command kept in communication with their outlying camps along the south coast. At Tsoutsouros on the South Coast, the walls of the Roman camp still remain.

One of the most fascinating features of Gortyn are the famous municipal Laws. These were inscribed around 565 B.C. and incorporated by the Romans into an odeum-or covered theatre. (G) Consisting of some 17000 characters carved on 12 columns, each with some 52 lines of Ancient Greek lettering with a Dorian dialect (Plate 27).

Few would have been able to read the Laws. Fewer still would have been able to understand them. Probably they were read aloud by an educated noble. The inscriber has carefully carved each alternate line in the opposite direction from the previous line. Thus from right to left, then from left to right. In consequence, the letters of the words in the lines from right to left are in mirror image. This style is known as 'boustrophedon' fashion or as the ox ploughs.

One cannot help but wonder if this was a deliberate attempt to make the laws even harder to understand! Did the unknown inscriber set a precedent for the legal documents of today?

The great Solon, (c. 640-560 B.C.) the Greek statesman and law maker, is said to have visited Gortyn and studied the Laws, though no record remains as to his reaction to them.

A large Minoan farmhouse has been discovered in the area of the acropolis. (H)

1. West Court or Theatrical Area
2. A shrine complex of the first palace
3. West Façade of the first palace
4. Corridor
5. Grand staircase
6. Propylaion
7. Magazines of the First palace with pithoi
8. Peristyle hall
9. Queen's apartment
10. Internal Court
11. Artisan's Rooms
12. Rooms with earlier Peristyle
13. Rooms with Hermaria
14. Workshops
15. Central Court Corridor
16. Central Court
17. Double line of Magazines
18. Pillared hall
19. Sanctuaries of the West Wing
20. Rooms with benches
21. Southwest Pillar and rooms
22. Portico with Columns on two sides
23. Probably Workshops
24. Hellenistic building including an Exedra
25. Lustral basin
26. A complex of rooms in which was discovered the Phaistos Disk.

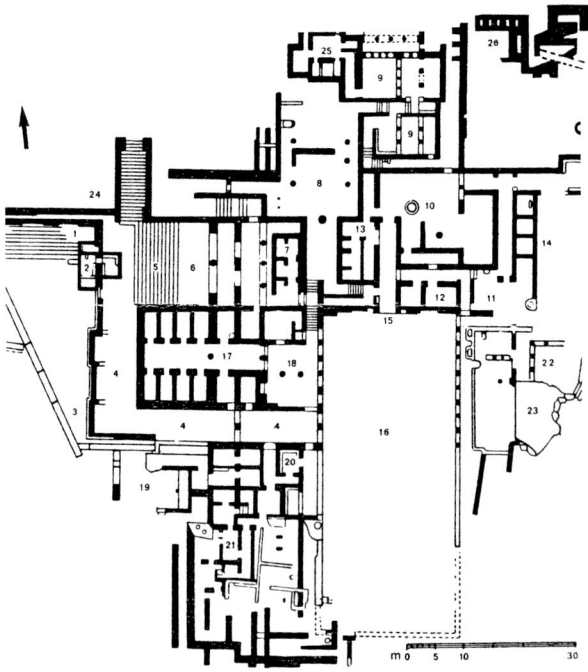

Fig. K. Plan of Phaistos

19 Palace of Phaistos

Set on a commanding hill at the western end of the fertile Messara plain, the inhabitants of the Palace of Phaistos enjoyed a view unequalled on the island.

Framed by the Ida mountains, the rich soil of the countryside stretches out in a profusion of olive trees and corn fields as far as the eye can see.

A good surfaced road winds its way up to the Palace making easy access to the site.

The majority of the buildings which one sees are from the Second Palace built after the great earthquake of 1730 B.C. but many traces of the First Palace remain and it is to these that we shall first direct our steps.

Skirting to the left of the other buildings, we head for the Shrine complex (2) and the West Facade (3) of the First Palace. These date back to c. 2000 B.C.

Moving around to the north of the palace, we approach the treasury of the First Palace and the small cists or chambers (26). It was in the first of these that the Phaistos Disk was discovered in 1908.

We now walk through the Queen's Apartments (9) of the later palace and into the Peristyle Hall (8). To our right can be seen the Grand Staircase.

Plate 28. Bowl from Phaistos.

Passing the Magazines (7) with its squat pithoi tightly wedged beneath a roof of concrete, we may wonder how anyone ever retrieved their contents. The pithoi were the storage containers of the First Palace and the contents spoiled in the earthquake. The concrete roof was put in position during the building of the Second Palace, after the earthquake.

We now come to the Pillared Hall (18) and from here enter the paved Central Courtyard (16). The stone block, possibly used by the 'Kneeling Bull' (See Section 6) during the bull-leaping events, lies in the north west corner of the courtyard.

From here it is possible under favourable conditions to see the entrance to the Kamares Cave, high up in the face of the Ida Mountain. It was there that large quantities of the distinctive 'Kamares ware' pottery were discovered.

At various places throughout the palace, traces of wall-paintings can be found, as can the distinctive mason's marks previously discussed (See Section 9).

Since 1901, the excavations have been carried out each season by the Italian school of Archaeology. The Museum at Heraklion displays all of the movable finds from Phaistos, including the Phaistos Disk and numerous ceramics of quality (Plate 28).

Plate 29. View over Triadha.

Plate 30. Storage Magazine.

20　Summer Palace at Triadha

Remains of a Minoan road connect the Palace of Phaistos and the Summer palace of Triadha. It was to Triadha some 3 km distant, that the Royal Household made their way to enjoy the view across to the sea and the slightly cooler climate. This delightful setting still retains a feeling of peace (Plate 29).

As we enter the site of the palace, a unique series of shops which date back to the times of the occupation by the Mycenaeans can be seen on our right. A large Minoan House with its own courtyard lies to our left.

Descending down steps, we approach the Mycenaean 'megaron', a distinctive feature of Mycenaean palaces, similar to those found at Pylos on the Peloponnese.

An interesting find are the storage magazines with the smashed pithoi bearing the scars of the final destruction of Triadha (Plate 30).

The 'sitting room' is still a delightful haven from the heat of the day and lies to the north of the magazines. Adjacent are the Archives, where a mass of tablets in Linear A script were discovered, and the Treasury. It was in the Treasury that nineteen bronze ingots were stored, each weighing one talent (29.5 Kg).

A craftsman of distinction supplied the inhabitants of Triadha with the products of his labours. Three marvellous pieces, the 'Boxer Vase', the 'Harvester Vase' and the 'Chieftain Cup', all originally of gold-covered steatite were found here. All provide an insight into the customs of the Minoans.

Another important find was the seal of Queen Tye, wife of the Egyptian Amenhotep III (1412-1376 B.C.). This enables the dating of the destruction of Triadha, to be placed with some certainly as after 1412 B.C.

Plate 31. Castle of Frangokastello.

Plate 32. Lion of St. Mark.

21   Frangokastello

Commanding the flat coastal plain that separates the mountains from the sea to the east of Chora Hakio, the Venetian castle built in 1371 A.D. stands remote and defiant (Plate 31).

In the height of the summer, the castle shimmers in the heat haze looking like a desert mirage. Its well preserved condition belies its age.

This castle of the Franks (Gk. foreigners) consists of a simple rectangular shaped layout of castellated walls. Strengthened towers connected by a continuous walkway can be seen at each of the four corners. This narrow walk was once patrolled by guards and lookouts.

The south-west tower adjacent to the Sea-gate, has been further strengthened with even thicker walls and is higher than the others. From the top of this tower which served as the last position of defence, approaching ships could easily be observed. Above the Sea Gate, the winged Lion of St. Mark can be seen fashioned in stone (Plate 32). Other heraldic devices flanked this emblem. Further coats-of-arms can be seen in the wall of this massive tower, where stone steps descend down to the level of the sea.

The walls of the castle show signs of repair work carried out over the ages since it was built. At regular intervals shaped embrasures have been cut through the walls. Normally these are wider on the inside allowing the defender of the castle the greatest possible field of view. This also limits the attacker's chances of penetrating the narrower outside opening. Here at Frangokastello, both the inside and the outside of the embrasures have been widened.

For many years the castle was used as a storage depot for the Venetian navy. The design of the embrasures affording the guards on the outside a better view of the vital stores. The internal walls of the Dining hall and minor storerooms still remain.

The Castle of Frangokastello and the adjoining sands are full of relics from the past. Many furious battles were fought here over the past centuries and the area once echoed to the cries of wounded men.

At certain times of the year, around dawn when the early morning mist is slowly stirred by the rising heat of the day, strange shapes can be seen entering the castle and moving around the walls. These dew-formed images, known as 'drossoulites' seem almost lifelike. One can easily imagine the glint of the sun on helmets and body armour.

At the far end of the wide shallow beach can be found the remains of the medieval village. The stub of the ancient windmill which used to grind the local corn can be seen. The large circular grinding mill stones now lie outside.

Such is the unspoilt peace of Frangokastello and the fine bathing facilities which can be enjoyed, that it is an ideal place to visit. Local buses frequent the area twice a day in the season. Tavernas and rooms are available for those wishing to stay overnight.

Plate 33. The Samaria Gorge.

22 Samaria Gorge

A full day should be allowed for the unforgettable walk through the gorge of Samaria. Descending from a height of 1227m. the gorge eventually emerges at sea-level at the coast near Agia Roumeli. The descent should not be commenced until the early morning mist has cleared from the head of the gorge. Good walking shoes should be worn. The initial descent of some 500 metres takes about 15 minutes using the adequate wooden steps which are installed. A pause at the bottom of the steps to ensure that all members of one's group are together, is recommended before proceeding through the gorge.

The Samaria Gorge is one of the few remaining places on the island where the visitor can occasionally catch a glimpse of the Cretan 'agrimi'. This is the species of wild goat whose forbears go back to Minoan times, and which is depicted on the 'Mountain Shrine' rhyton from Zakros.

The gorge, the longest in Europe is some 18 Kms. in length and takes some 5-6 hours to traverse. It narrows from some 40m. to a mere 5m. at the 'siderportes' - iron doors (Plate 33), where the sheer height of the walls almost blocks out the sky. In the middle of the gorge the deserted village of Samaria is passed. During the winter months, the combination of the melting snow and the rain makes the gorge impassable. Even in summer the flowing river must be crossed many times throughout the journey.

The sudden view of the sea beyond the pebbled beach is as startling as it is welcomed. Small boats are waiting to transport walkers to Chora Sfakion. At this little harbour village, those who travelled by coach from their hotels to the head of the gorge, will find their coaches waiting for them.

23 Paleochora

For many visitors to the island of Crete, the coastal town of Paleochora caters for their every need. Situated on the south coast and with frequent transport from the north, the town is easily accessible.

Its long wide sandy beaches and sheltering trees are a mecca for many young people, whilst hotel and other accomodation is available for those who do not wish to "sleep under the stars".

The town provides bookshops, discos, bars, kiosks, travel agents, supermarkets, garages and banks. Fresh baked bread and local honey is also available. The High Street which during the day provides access to these various facilities, becomes a meeting place in the evenings. Free from traffic, the many tavernas on either side of the street move their tables across the road and throng with holiday makers meeting old friends and making new ones.

A Venetian castle provides the theatrical setting for the local dramatic society. During the season they perform Greek plays in the early evening. Along the eastern end of the sea-front promenade, much of which is newly renovated, many tavernas serve dinner at tables overlooking the beach. Whilst to the west of Paleochora, mile upon mile of secluded bays with smooth beaches are available for those preferring a quieter situation.

The well-surfaced serpentine road to Paleochora via Kandanos is an experience in itself with magnificent views across the Libyan Sea towards the coast of Africa. Travellers approaching Paleochora via Voutas will have found the road surfaces 'surprising' to say the least. Taken with a certain degree of caution, all are passable. Motorists with high vehicles should pause and consider and alternative route before attempting to drive through the unlit tunnel, south of Topolia.

Victor J. Kean is a freelance writer specialising in archaeology, history and travel. The first of his archaeological works, "The Disk from Phaistos" was published in 1985 and was followed by the intriguing story of the "Antikythera Mechanism", the ancient Greek computer. Now he has written the first in a new series entitled "CRETE - New light on Old Mysteries" which provides a guide to the island's history and an introduction to some of the lesser known delights which await the visitor.

Other works in this series:

2) "Rhodes"
3) "Kerkyra" (Corfu)